Helen Exley Giftbooks
for the most thoughtful gifts of all

OTHER BOOKS IN THIS SERIES:
For a wonderful Mother A book to make your own
For a real Friend A book to make your own
A Girl's Journal A personal notebook and keepsake
A Woman's Journal A personal notebook and keepsake
Teddy Bears A book to make your own
Inspirations A book to make your own
A Gardener's Journal A book to make your own
For a wonderful Grandmother A book to make your own
OTHER HELEN EXLEY GIFTBOOKS
ON PETS:
Cat Quips!
The Littlest Cat Book
Glorious Cats
Dog Quotations

Published in hardback 1990. Published in softcover 2001.
Copyright © Helen Exley 1990, 2001
Selection © Helen Exley 1990, 2001
The moral right of the author has been asserted.

12 11 10 9 8 7 6 5 4 3 2

ISBN 1-86187-212-7

Selection and design by Helen Exley
Illustrated by Juliette Clarke
Printed in China

Exley Publications Ltd, 16 Chalk Hill, Watford, Herts, WD1 4BN, UK.
Exley Publications LLC, 232 Madison Avenue, Suite 1409, NY 10016, USA.

Acknowledgements: The publishers are grateful for permission to reproduce copyright material. Whilst every reasonable effort has been made to trace copyright holders, we would be pleased to hear from any not here acknowledged. Celia Haddon: From *The Love of Cats* published by Headline Books © 1992 Celia Haddon. Reprinted with permission of Curtis Brown. Dilys Laing: "Miao" from *In Praise of Cats*, published by Smithmark, 1992. John Richard Stephens: From *The Enchanted Cat* © 1990, Prima Publishing, Roseville, CA, USA.

Cats

A BOOK TO
MAKE YOUR OWN

A HELEN EXLEY
GIFTBOOK

EXLEY
NEW YORK • WATFORD, UK

$\mathcal{A}$ morning kiss, a discreet touch of his nose
landing somewhere on the middle of my face.
Because his long white whiskers tickled,
I began every day laughing.

JANET F. FAURE

He lies there, purring and dreaming, shifting his limbs

now and then in an ecstasy of cushioned comfort.

He seems the incarnation of everything soft and silky and velvety,

without a sharp edge in his composition, a dreamer

whose philosophy is sleep and let sleep....

SAKI (1870-1916)

$\mathscr{I}$ put down my book
"The Meaning of Zen"
and see the cat
smiling into her fur
as she delicately combs it
with her rough pink tongue.
"Cat, I would lend you
this book to study
but it appears
that you have already read it."
She looks up
and gives me her full gaze.
"Don't be ridiculous,"
she purrs.
"I wrote it."

DILYS LAING, "MIAO"

*B*less their little pointed faces
and their big, loyal hearts.
If a cat did not put a firm paw down
now and then, how could his human
remain possessed?

WINIFRED CARRIÈRE

CATS, AS A CLASS, HAVE NEVER COMPLETELY GOT OVER THE
SNOOTINESS CAUSED BY THE FACT THAT IN
ANCIENT EGYPT THEY WERE WORSHIPPED AS GODS.

P.G. WODEHOUSE (1881-1975)

A kitten is so flexible she is almost double;

the hind parts are equivalent to another kitten

with which the forepart plays.

She does not discover that her tail belongs to her

until you tread on it.

HENRY DAVID THOREAU (1817-1862)

I think that the reason that we admire cats,
those of us who do, is their proficiency in one-upmanship.
They always seem to come up on top, no matter
what they are doing – or pretend to be doing.

BARBARA WEBSTER

*They taught the children the lesson of the necessity
of kindness to smaller, weaker creatures.
But mostly they were just there: warm breath, furry lives,
acute intelligence, carriers of optimism and faith....*

NANCY THAYER

One small cat changes coming home to an empty house to coming home.

PAM BROWN, B.1928

Stately, kindly, lordly friend.
Condescend
Here to sit by me, and turn
Glorious eyes that smile and burn,
Golden eyes, love's lustrous meed,
On the golden page I read.

All your wondrous wealth of hair,
Dark and fair,
Silken-shaggy, soft and bright
As the clouds and beams of night,
Pays my reverent hand's caress
Back with friendlier gentleness....

ALGERNON CHARLES SWINBURNE
(1837-1909)

He was very imperious; very definite and autocratic in his requirements. He really needed a vassal, dedicated to his service alone....

MARGUERITE STEEN

... cats have a way of endearing themselves to their owners, not just by their "kittenoid" behaviour, which stimulates strong parental feelings, but also by their sheer gracefulness. There is an elegance and a composure about them that captivates the human eye. To the sensitive human being it becomes a privilege to share a room with a cat, exchange its glance, feel its greeting rub, or watch it gently luxuriate itself into a snoozing ball on a soft cushion.

DESMOND MORRIS, B.1928,
FROM "CATWATCHING AND CATLORE"

*I*n these days of tension,
human beings can learn a great deal
about relaxation from watching a cat,
who doesn't just lie down
when it is time to rest,
but pours his body on the floor
and rests in every
nerve and muscle.

MURRAY ROBINSON

THE SMALLEST FELINE IS A MASTERPIECE.

LEONARDO DA VINCI (1452-1519)

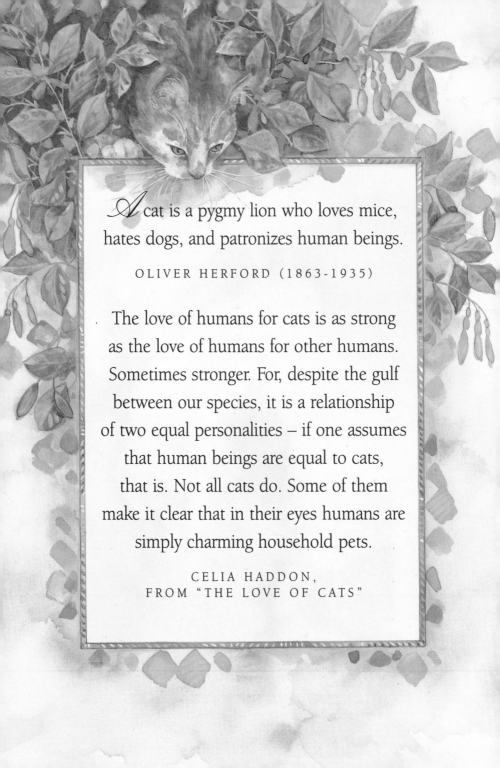

$\mathscr{A}$ cat is a pygmy lion who loves mice, hates dogs, and patronizes human beings.

OLIVER HERFORD (1863-1935)

The love of humans for cats is as strong as the love of humans for other humans. Sometimes stronger. For, despite the gulf between our species, it is a relationship of two equal personalities – if one assumes that human beings are equal to cats, that is. Not all cats do. Some of them make it clear that in their eyes humans are simply charming household pets.

CELIA HADDON,
FROM "THE LOVE OF CATS"

*... when she walked... she stretched out long and thin
like a little tiger, and held her head high
to look over the grass as if she were threading the jungle.*

SARAH ORNE JEWETT (1849-1909)

$\mathcal{T}$he great charm of cats
is their rampant egotism,
their devil-may-care attitude
toward responsibility,
their disinclination to earn
an honest dollar...
cats are disdainful of everything
but their own
immediate interests....

ROBERTSON DAVIES, B.1913

*There is little question but that cats are born to the purple.
Unlike people, they do not undergo the vulgar period of
the nouveau riche but take instantaneously to the luxuries of life
with elegant aplomb.*

VIVIAN CRISTOL

... THEY [CATS] ARE REMARKABLE ANIMALS;
THEY'RE NOT LIKE ANYTHING ELSE – THEY'RE EXTREMELY GOOD
FOR ANYONE WHO IS EXCITABLE OR WHO HAS HEART TROUBLE
OR HIGH BLOOD PRESSURE. THEY ARE WONDERFULLY SOOTHING
TO BE WITH, AND THEY'RE VERY VERY RESTFUL.

BERYL REID, B.1920, FROM "A PASSION FOR CATS"

$\mathcal{A}$ cat is a lion in a jungle of small bushes.

INDIAN PROVERB

$\mathcal{I}$t is impossible for a lover of cats
to banish these alert and discriminating little friends,
who give us just enough of their regard
and compliance to make us hunger for more.

AGNES REPPLIER

The greater cats with golden eyes
Stare out between the bars.
Deserts are there, and different skies,
And night with different stars.

VITA SACKVILLE-WEST

As all cat-loving families have found, cats are indeed catalysts – mellowing human moods, perceptibly changing the impression and atmosphere of any room they have chosen to inhabit. They contribute immeasurably to the lives of countless people, to whom they are friends and confidants.

MARTYN LEWIS, FROM "CATS IN THE NEWS"

Cats fill in all the empty spaces in the human world. The comfortable ones.

MARION C. GARRETTY, B.1917

A kitten
is a lethal weapon
disguised as
a cute fluffy bundle
of joy.

STUART AND LINDA MACFARLANE

*You can't look
at a sleeping cat
and feel tense.*

JANE PAULEY

$\mathcal{D}$OGS COME WHEN THEY ARE CALLED;
CATS TAKE A MESSAGE AND GET BACK TO YOU.

MARY BLY

... anyone who goes through the years indifferent to the beauty,
the elegance, the ingenuity, the intelligence, the affection
of which the cat is capable – such a person is as impoverished
as one who, while walking along a country lane in summer,
is blind to the flowers in the hedgerow, deaf to the song of birds,
the hum of insects, the whisper of leaves in the wind.

ELIZABETH HAMILTON, FROM "CATS A CELEBRATION"

Very few people
have the opportunity to know a wild animal
as a friend.
Except, that is, for our cats.

MARION C. GARRETTY, B.1917

It always gives me a shiver when I see a cat seeing what I can't see.

ELEANOR FARJEON (1881-1965)

Cats will always lie soft.

THEOCRITUS
(c. 310-250 B.C.)

$\mathcal{G}$ive her but a wavering leaf-shadow of a breeze
combing the grasses and she was back a million years,
glaring with night-lit eyes in the thickets,
projecting a terrible aura of fear that stilled and quelled
all creatures.

PAUL ANNIXTER

A cat does not leap up at you,
or lick your face all over or run mad circles round you,
making hysterical noises.
It meets you at the door and leans very softly against your legs
and reverberates.

PAM BROWN B.1928

Cats lack our preconceived notions
of what the world is all about.
Oblivious to the cares,
worries, and desires that plague us,
they sit back and watch the world,
observing without making judgments,
rather like small furry Buddhas.
Maybe it's this Zen outlook
that attracts us to cats.
They accept us as we are,
without passing judgment.

JOHN RICHARD STEPHENS,
FROM "THE ENCHANTED CAT"

... he is an instrument for the children
to learn benevolence upon.
For every house is incomplete
without him.

CHRISTOPHER SMART (1722-1771),
FROM "JUBILATE AGNO"

French novelist Colette was a firm cat-lover.
When she was in the U.S. she saw a cat....
She went over to talk to it and the two of them mewed at each
other for a friendly minute. Colette turned to her
companion and exclaimed,
"Enfin! Quelqu'un qui parle français."
(At last! Someone who speaks French!).

ANON

Human beings are drawn to cats
because they are all we are not
– self-contained, elegant in everything they do,
relaxed, assured, glad of company,
yet still possessing secret lives.

PAM BROWN, B.1928

*Sometimes he will sit in front of you
with eyes so melting,
so caressing and so human,
that they almost frighten you,
for it is impossible to believe
that a soul is not there.*

THEOPHILE GAUTIER (1811-1872)

... THE HAUGHTY, THE UNCONQUERED,

THE MYSTERIOUS, THE LUXURIOUS,

THE BABYLONIAN, THE IMPERSONAL,

THE ETERNAL COMPANION OF

SUPERIORITY AND ART — THE TYPE OF PERFECT

BEAUTY AND THE BROTHER OF POETRY — THE

BLAND, GRAVE, COMPETENT, AND PATRICIAN CAT.

H.P. LOVECRAFT (1890-1937)